No More Excuses —
A New Approach To Tackling
Youth Crime In
England And Wales

PRESENTED TO PARLIAMENT BY THE SECRETARY OF STATE FOR THE HOME DEPARTMENT

BY COMMAND OF HER MAJESTY.

NOVEMBER 1997.

CM 3809

£7.10

NO MORE EXCUSES —
A NEW APPROACH TO TACKLING
YOUTH CRIME IN
ENGLAND AND WALES

This White Paper seeks to draw a line under the past and sets out a new approach to tackling youth crime. It begins the root and branch reform of the youth justice system that the Government promised the public before the Election. It will deliver our Manifesto pledge to halve the time it takes to get persistent young offenders from arrest to sentencing.

All those working in the youth justice system must have a principal aim - to prevent offending. That will be the statutory aim we set out for them in the new Crime and Disorder Bill. With Final Warnings instead of repeat cautions, new action plan, reparation and parenting orders, and a new national network of Youth Offending Teams providing programmes to stop offending behaviour, we are putting in place the means of delivering this aim. To give more strategic direction, set standards and measure performance, the Government will set up a new Youth Justice Board for England and Wales.

Today's young offenders can too easily become tomorrow's hardened criminals. As a society we do ourselves no favours by failing to break the link between juvenile crime and disorder and the serial burglar of the future. For too long we have assumed that young offenders will grow out of their offending if left to themselves. The research evidence shows this does not happen.

We are determined to cut out the waste in the present youth justice system as identified by the Audit Commission last year. Instead we will refocus resources and the talents of professionals on nipping offending in the bud, to prevent crime from becoming a way of life for so many young people.

An excuse culture has developed within the youth justice system. It excuses itself for its inefficiency, and too often excuses the young offenders before it, implying that they cannot help their behaviour because of their social circumstances. Rarely are they confronted with their behaviour and helped to take more personal responsibility for their actions. The system allows them to go on wrecking their own lives as well as disrupting their families and communities.

JACK STRAW
November 1997

INTRODUCTION

This White Paper sets out the Government's programme of reform for the youth justice system in England and Wales. The reform programme aims to provide:

- a clear strategy to prevent offending and re-offending (chapters 2 and 3)
- that offenders, and their parents, face up to their offending behaviour and take responsibility for it (chapter 4)
- earlier, more effective intervention when young people first offend (chapters 5 and 6)
- faster, more efficient procedures from arrest to sentence (chapter 7)
- partnership between all youth justice agencies to deliver a better, faster system (chapter 8).

These measures will be taken forward through the Crime and Disorder Bill in the current Parliamentary session. The Government also sees a need for more fundamental reform to change the culture of the youth court, making it more open and accessible, engaging offenders and their families more closely and giving a greater voice to victims. Proposals are set out – for consultation – in chapter 9.

A clear strategy to prevent offending

As well as putting the public at risk, allowing young people to drift into a life of crime undermines their welfare and denies them the opportunity to develop into fully contributing members of society. The Government believes that the purpose of the youth justice system must be to help prevent offending by the young people with which it deals.

The Crime and Disorder Bill will provide a clear focus on preventing offending by establishing this in statute as the **aim of the youth justice system** and by placing a statutory **duty on youth justice agencies** to have regard to the need to prevent offending by young people (chapter 2). The aim and duty will be supported by non-statutory objectives and a new protocol, on which the Government would welcome views.

A range of initiatives is underway across Government to tackle the causes of crime (chapter 3). The Crime and Disorder Bill will introduce statutory local partnerships, led by local authorities and the police, to harness the efforts of communities to reduce crime and disorder. Wherever youth crime is a particular local problem, it should be addressed in the local crime reduction strategy.

Taking responsibility

To prevent offending and re-offending by young people, we must stop making excuses for youth crime. Children above the age of criminal responsibility are generally mature enough to be accountable for their actions and the law should recognise this. Chapter 4 sets out plans to abolish the English common law presumption of **doli incapax** and for requiring more young offenders to make reparation to their victims, including through a new **reparation order**.

Parents have a crucial role in preventing their children committing criminal and anti-social acts. Chapter 4 sets out ways of reinforcing parents' responsibilities through a new **parenting order** to help parents turn their children away from crime.

Earlier, more effective intervention

The Milton Keynes youth justice audit, published in February 1995, concluded that "much of the effort put into the system is 'processing', with...very little indeed on 'preventing crime' or 'service' [to victims, offenders and witnesses]"[1]. The Government shares this view. It believes that the efforts of the youth justice system are currently weighted too heavily towards dealing with young offenders whose behaviour has been allowed to escalate out of control, rather than intervening early and effectively to prevent and reduce crime and anti-social behaviour.

There will be a new focus on nipping crime in the bud – stopping children at risk from getting involved in crime and preventing early criminal behaviour from escalating into persistent or serious offending. Chapter 5 sets out new local authority, police and court powers to protect young children from being drawn into criminal and anti-social behaviour – the **child safety** order and the **local child curfew**.

Cautioning for young offenders will be replaced by a new police reprimand and **Final Warning** scheme (chapter 5). Community intervention programmes will follow for offenders receiving a Final Warning, to address offending behaviour and try to turn them away from crime before they end up in court.

A new community punishment will be introduced to help prevent re-offending. The **action plan order** (chapter 5) will combine punishment, reparation and rehabilitation.

If community intervention does not work, and for young offenders found guilty of serious crimes, custodial penalties are necessary to protect the public. Public protection is best served if punishment is combined with rehabilitation so that young offenders are equipped to lead law-abiding and useful lives once they are released from custody.

A new **detention and training order** will combine custody and community supervision to punish and rehabilitate youngsters whose crimes require secure detention. The Government will also give courts clear powers to remand juveniles to secure accommodation where this is necessary to protect the public and prevent further offending (chapter 6).

Faster, more efficient procedures

Delays in the youth justice system can frustrate and anger victims and give young offenders the impression that they can offend with impunity. The Government's top priority is to halve the time taken for persistent young offenders to get from arrest to sentence.

Delays will be cut by introducing **streamlined procedures** and **better case management** and by setting **mandatory time limits** for all criminal proceedings involving young people (chapter 7). Strict time limits for persistent young offenders, backed by performance targets, will ensure fast-track justice and a speedy response to the offending of those individuals from whom the public most needs protection.

Partnership

The Government believes clear national leadership is necessary to improve the performance of the youth justice system. A new **Youth Justice Board** for England and Wales will be established to advise Ministers on setting standards for service delivery and to monitor performance (chapter 8).

Dealing effectively with young offenders requires that different agencies pool their skills and co-operate at a local level. Chapter 8 explains the new duty which is to be placed on local authorities with social services and education responsibilities to ensure the provision of inter-agency **Youth Offending Teams** in their areas.

Further reform

Chapter 9 sets out proposals for further **reform of the youth court**, to provide a faster, more open system, with a less adversarial approach. The new arrangements would engage young people and their parents in preventing offending and give an opportunity to victims to be heard.

CONSULTATION

The Government would welcome views in response to:

- **the proposals in chapter 2 for a protocol to support the statutory duty of youth justice agencies to have regard to the need to prevent offending; and**

- **the proposals in chapter 9 for reform of the youth court.**

Responses should be sent, by the end of March 1998, to:

Nicole Smith
Juvenile Offenders Unit
Home Office
50, Queen Anne's Gate
LONDON SW1H 9AT

The Government may be asked to publish responses to this White Paper. Please let us know if you do not want your response to be published.

Crime and Disorder Bill

CHAPTER 2
- aim of youth justice system and duty on agencies to have regard to it

CHAPTER 4
- abolition of doli incapax
- reparation order
- parenting order

CHAPTER 5
- child safety order
- local child curfew
- Final Warning scheme
- action plan order
- amendments to the supervision order

CHAPTER 6
- detention and training order
- new arrangements for secure remands of 12-16 year olds

CHAPTER 7
- streamlined procedures
- statutory time limits

CHAPTER 8
- Youth Justice Board for England and Wales
- Youth Offending Teams
- duties on local authorities and other agencies to ensure availability of appropriate youth justice services

PROPOSALS ON WHICH

COMMENTS WOULD BE

WELCOMED

CHAPTER 2
- fuller non-statutory protocol setting out how agencies should deliver the aim of the youth justice system alongside their existing duties

CHAPTER 9
- reforming the youth court

PART I - The problem

Chapter 1

The facts

about youth crime

What do we know about juvenile crime?

1.1   Home Office research shows that among 14-25 year olds, one in two males and one in three females admits to having committed an offence[2]. The Audit Commission estimated in 1996 that people under 18 commit 7 million offences a year[3]. 1996 statistics for offenders convicted or cautioned for an indictable offence show that 10-15 year olds account for around 14% of known offenders, and 10-17 year olds account for around 25%[4].

1.2   The great majority of young people who commit offences do so infrequently. But a small hard core of persistent offenders is responsible for a disproportionate amount of crime. Home Office research has found that about 3% of young offenders commit 26% of youth crime[2]. Figures for 1995 show that 0.3% of males born in 1973 had six or more court appearances by age 17 and accounted for 21% of all court appearances for that age group[5].

1.3   Most offences committed by young offenders are property crimes. But, worryingly, between 1985 and 1995 known offending rates for robbery and drugs offences have increased substantially[6].

What are the causes of youth crime?

1.4   There is no easy link of cause and effect between the factors associated with youth crime and actual offending. A range of risk factors is involved – which might include psychological, family, social, economic and cultural factors, plus of course the opportunity to commit an offence. These risks may be offset by positive influences such as good parenting. Crime does not happen in a social vacuum. It is correlated with social disadvantage and poverty. People living in deprived circumstances are at greater risk of being perpetrators — and victims — of crime. However, a simplistic, deterministic view of the causes of crime is not supported by the facts and risks both insulting those in deprived circumstances who do not commit offences and making excuses for those who do.

1.5   We know a good deal about the factors which are associated with youth crime. Research[2] has confirmed that key factors related to youth criminality are:

- being male;
- being brought up by a criminal parent or parents;
- living in a family with multiple problems;
- experiencing poor parenting and lack of supervision;
- poor discipline in the family and at school;
- playing truant or being excluded from school;
- associating with delinquent friends; and
- having siblings who offend.

1.6   Two important influences are persistent school truancy and associating with offenders, but the single most important factor in explaining criminality is the quality of a young person's home life, including parental supervision.

Different for girls?

1.7   According to statistics based on crimes which have been resolved by the police, the great majority of juvenile crime – like adult crime – is committed by males. There were 142,600 males aged 10-17 convicted or cautioned in 1996 and only 34,400 females[6].

1.8   Self-report data reveals a more complex picture. The Home Office study *Young People and Crime*[2] showed the ratio of males to females who admitted they had ever committed an offence was nearly 1:1 for 14-17 year olds (although the number and seriousness of self-reported offences was significantly greater for boys). The ratio of male to female offenders increased to 4:1 for 18-21 year olds and to 11:1 for young adults aged 22-25.

Just a phase?

1.9   A prevailing assumption behind youth justice policy has been the idea that youngsters will grow out of their offending behaviour. For many young offenders it is true that their first caution – or court appearance – is enough to divert them from crime. But this assumption is wide of the mark when it comes to the hard core of persistent offenders who cause so much crime.

1.10   While many young offenders do grow out of their delinquent behaviour, research shows that this happens less markedly and far more slowly for young men than young women. For young men, the positive effects of personal and social development – completing education, getting a job, leaving home, settling down with a partner – tend to be outweighed by the more powerful influences of the peer group and siblings. Desistance from offending is even less likely for young male offenders involved in regular drug or alcohol misuse[2].

1.11   The peak age of self-reported offending for males is 21 and for females, 16[2]. For males identified by the police and courts, the peak age of offending has increased over the last decade from 15 to 18 years[7]. The number of 18-20 year olds will increase by one sixth over the next ten years[8], so if effective action is not taken, crime committed by young adult males is likely to increase. Many of today's juvenile offenders may graduate into tomorrow's adult criminals unless action is taken now.

Young people are also victims

1.12   Young people do not only commit crime disproportionately. They suffer from it disproportionately. When the British Crime Survey (BCS) questioned 12-15 year olds in 1992, nearly 20% reported having experienced a crime in the last six months[9]. The Audit Commission showed in 1996 that young people were more likely to be victims of personal crime than adults[3]. Young people are generally at greater risk of all types of violence than older people: according to the 1996 BCS[10], almost 21% of men aged 16-25 reported being victims of violent crime, as against 4% of men aged 26 or above. 11% of women aged 16-25 years old reported being the victim of some kind of violent crime, but less than 3% of women aged 26 or above. Young people themselves have an interest in tackling offending both by their peers and by older people

What works to prevent crime?

1.13   We know that those who start committing offences at an early age are more likely to become serious and persistent offenders[11]. So the Government's youth justice reforms will focus efforts on preventing offending, on early and effective intervention to stop children and young people being drawn into crime and, if they are, to halt their offending before it escalates.

PART II - PREVENTING YOUTH CRIME

CHAPTER 2

THE AIM OF YOUTH JUSTICE SYSTEM

What is the system for?

2.1 In the past, the youth justice system has suffered from changing policy priorities and a lack of consistent direction. The Government believes that there has been confusion about the purpose of the youth justice system and the principles that should govern the way in which young people are dealt with by youth justice agencies. Concerns about the welfare of the young person have too often been seen as in conflict with the aims of protecting the public, punishing offences and preventing offending. This confusion creates real practical difficulties for practitioners and has contributed to the loss of public confidence in the youth justice system.

2.2 Children need protection as appropriate from the full rigour of criminal law. Under the UN Convention on the Rights of the Child and the European Convention on Human Rights, the United Kingdom is committed to protecting the welfare of children and young people who come into contact with the criminal justice process. The Government does not accept that there is any conflict between protecting the welfare of a young offender and preventing that individual from offending again. Preventing offending promotes the welfare of the individual young offender and protects the public.

2.3 The different youth justice agencies have different roles and in some cases different professional and statutory responsibilities to uphold. But all agencies dealing with young offenders also have a responsibility to deliver the aims of the youth justice system of which they are part. Preventing offending by young people is a key aim: it is in the best interests of the young person and the public.

A duty on youth justice agencies

2.4 Accordingly, the Crime and Disorder Bill will make clear that the aim of the youth justice system is to prevent offending by young people. The Bill will place a duty on all people working in the youth justice system to have regard to that aim.

2.5 The new duty will cover all youth justice agencies across England and Wales—i.e. the police, the probation service, social services, others working in Youth Offending Teams (see chapter 8), the Crown Prosecution Service, defence solicitors, the Prison Service and courts—in their dealings with young people. It will help to provide unity of purpose and coherence of effort. The new duty will be complemented by the Government's proposals for a new Youth Justice Board for England and Wales to advise on setting standards and monitor performance (see chapter 8).

2.6 The new duty to have regard to the aim of the youth justice system will not supersede practitioners' existing functions but will encourage them to consider how their actions and decisions when dealing with young people can help prevent offending. Avoiding unnecessary delays, for example, can reduce the chances of offending while awaiting sentence; and encouraging young people to face up to the consequences of their offending behaviour can help change patterns of behaviour, as can community and custodial penalties which focus clearly on the causes of offending and which are properly enforced.

2.7 This clear focus on preventing offending by young people will reinforce measures in the Crime and Disorder Bill to place new duties on local authorities and the police in partnership to prepare strategies for reducing local crime and disorder.

How should we reinforce the duty on youth justice agencies?

2.8   The Government proposes that the aim of the youth justice system and the duty on youth justice practitioners should be supported by a fuller, non-statutory, set of objectives for youth justice agencies.

2.9   These objectives would build on proposals made by the Home Secretary's Youth Justice Task Force (an advisory group comprising a range of people with varied experience of the youth justice system, including victim issues, plus representatives of relevant Government Departments). The Task Force has proposed that the aim of preventing offending by young people should be achieved through the following objectives:

- the swift administration of justice so that every young person accused of breaking the law has the matter resolved without delay;
- confronting young offenders with the consequences of their offending, for themselves and their family, their victims and their community;
- punishment proportionate to the seriousness and persistence of offending;
- encouraging reparation to victims by young offenders;
- reinforcing the responsibilities of parents; and
- helping young offenders to tackle problems associated with their offending and to develop a sense of personal responsibility.

2.10   The Government proposes that non-statutory objectives for the youth justice system should be supported by a more detailed protocol drawn up in consultation with the relevant agencies and associations. The protocol would set out how the agencies should work together to meet the objectives and offer guidance on how to deliver the aim of preventing youth crime alongside existing statutory and non-statutory duties (for example, Crown Prosecutors' duties under the Prosecution of Offences Act 1985 to review cases in accordance with public interest and other criteria, and sentencers' obligations to follow the sentencing framework set out in the Criminal Justice Act 1991).

2.11   The protocol would provide a new start for youth justice agencies in England and Wales, providing the opportunity for a clear focus on preventing offending.

> **The Government would welcome views on the proposals in paragraphs 2.8-2.11.**

CHAPTER 3

TACKLING THE CAUSES OF YOUTH CRIME

3.1 At the moment, not enough is done to prevent children and young people becoming involved in criminal and anti-social behaviour. If we are serious about preventing youth crime, then action must start early and must be targeted where it is likely to be most effective.

3.2 It is neither possible nor desirable for the Government to involve itself in every aspect of family life or to dictate to parents how to raise their children: parents hold the primary responsibility for giving children the love and care they need, ensuring their welfare and security and teaching them right from wrong. But the Government can and should help parents to recognise and meet those responsibilities – and should strive to create the conditions in which families can flourish and all children have the chance to succeed. This chapter outlines Government initiatives to prevent youth crime and combat its causes.

Government-wide initiatives: restoring hope and opportunity

3.4 The Government is taking action across the board to help secure healthy communities and strong families and so give all children real opportunities, through:

- measures to support families including assistance for single parents to get off benefits and return to work, to help prevent marriage and family breakdown and to deal with such breakdown, if it does occur, with the least possible damage to any children. A new Ministerial group is being chaired by the Home Secretary to develop policies in support of the family and improve the co-ordination of Government effort;

- a determined assault on social exclusion with a new Cabinet Office unit, led by the Prime Minister, to recommend – in partnership with local government, the voluntary sector and business – new ways of ensuring that all have a chance to share in the benefits of economic success;

- policies to help children achieve at school, including: good quality nursery education for all 4 year olds (and progressively for 3 year olds too); higher school standards, with a particular focus on literacy and numeracy skills in primary schools; steps to tackle truancy and prevent so many exclusions; study support out of school hours; and better links between schools and business to help young people make the transition to adult working life;

- providing real opportunities for jobs, training, and leisure, through the New Start strategy aimed at re-engaging in education or training youngsters up to 17 who have switched off or dropped out; through the welfare to work New Deal for unemployed 18-24 year olds; through stable, sustainable economic growth and through positive leisure opportunities, including those which involve young people themselves in preventing crime; and

- action to tackle drug misuse with new initiatives in the criminal justice system, innovative projects showing what schools and the wider community can do and through the work of the new UK Anti-Drugs Co-ordinator in putting forward a new strategy aimed at young people.

3.5   These are all necessary and desirable social policies in their own right. They are also ways of helping to tackle the roots of juvenile crime. Action to address the causes of truancy and youth unemployment, for example, should also reduce the risk of youngsters becoming involved in crime, since:

- Home Office research shows that the odds of offending for youngsters who truant from school are three times higher than for those who do not and there is similarly a strong correlation between school exclusions and offending[2]; and

- figures for 1995 show that nearly 60% of convicted youths aged 16 or 17 were unemployed and not in training or education at the time that they were sentenced, when for 16 and 17 year olds in general, the proportion unemployed and not it training or education was only 12%[6].

Existing youth crime prevention

3.6   There is also a need for targeted youth crime prevention. The Government intends to build on and strengthen existing initiatives such as:

- Grants for Education Support and Training, which in 1997-98 will provide £1.5 million to support drug education and crime prevention programmes;

- the Home Office-sponsored Safer Cities programmes and Crime Concern's youth crime prevention work, including Youth Action Groups which involve young people in tackling problems such as bullying, graffiti, vandalism and drug misuse. Crime Concern's work is partly funded by an annual Government grant of £750,000; and

- work with the National Neighbourhood Watch Association and the National Association for the Care and Resettlement of Offenders to encourage young people to be part of the solution to crime, not part of the problem.

Existing local youth crime prevention partnerships include:

- **Warrington youth action partnership which aims to establish Youth Action Groups in Warrington and develop a long-term crime and drug prevention strategy. It involves the police, Crime Concern, social and youth services and many other local agencies and voluntary organisations; and**

- **Merton youth partnership against crime – the Community Safety Co-ordinator and local training and enterprise council have helped local high schools providing education on crime and citizenship. Young people are set projects such as conducting crime audits and arranging debates on drug problems.**

Getting to grips with crime – locally

3.7   Good local crime prevention schemes require effective co-operation between local agencies, with the support of the local community. The Crime and Disorder Bill will contain measures to ensure that local partnerships exist across England and Wales to combat local problems of crime and disorder and to see that local people can have their say. Proposals were set out in the consultation document *Getting to Grips with Crime – A New Framework for Local Action* for:

- a new joint duty on local authorities and the police to establish statutory partnerships to prevent and reduce crime and disorder. Partnerships' strategies will be developed in response to local problems, so the Government expects that measures to tackle youth crime will figure wherever that is a problem locally; and

- a new duty on local authorities to consider the crime and disorder implications of all policies.

Tackling drug and alcohol misuse

3.8   The Government also plans new measures to tackle problems which are closely linked to juvenile crime. Drugs and alcohol do not just damage the health of young misusers – they can seriously disrupt a child's education; lead to anti-social and disorderly behaviour and perhaps a lifetime of criminality; and can destroy families and communities.

Underage drinking

3.9   The Government is concerned by the prevalence of underage drinking, and the emergence of products like 'alcopops' which are popular among underage drinkers. The Government expects the drinks industry to take effective action against the sale of alcohol to minors and has set up a Ministerial Group to review the industry's response.

3.10   The Government has implemented new powers for police to confiscate alcohol from children in public and has undertaken both to change the law to allow test purchases for the purpose of enforcement and to prohibit irresponsible adults from buying alcohol on behalf of children.

3.11   Measures in the Crime and Disorder Bill will help youngsters whose offending is linked to alcohol or drugs misuse to break their habit and turn away from crime. New community interventions will address the factors contributing to a young person's offending (see chapter 5), including alcohol or drug misuse. The Bill will also pave the way for a network of new inter-agency Youth Offending Teams (YOTs) across England and Wales to tackle offending (see chapter 8). Every YOT will include a representative from the local health authority, to ensure that expertise on alcohol, drug and mental health problems is accessible to those dealing with young offenders in every area. YOTs will need to work with local Drug Action Teams and their reference groups, recognising their complementary roles.

Helping youngsters beat drugs

3.12.   Involvement in drug use among young people is widespread – one in two males and one in three females aged 14-25 admits to having tried illegal drugs[2]. Many even younger children have also experimented with drugs.

3.13   Most of those who try drugs will not go on to become regular users. Recently published British Crime Survey results indicate that the number of those who do has been roughly stable for at least the last two years[12]. But the numbers involved are still worryingly high and the younger the age at which children start to experiment, the more likely it is that they will go on to develop a serious drugs problem.

3.14   The new UK Anti-Drugs Co-ordinator is working with Ministers to draw up a new drugs strategy, based firmly on evidence about what works and on analysis of the underlying causes of drug misuse. Within the overall framework of vigorous law-enforcement and effective education, prevention and treatment measures, the strategy will recognise the links between drug misuse, social deprivation and crime and the need to reduce demand among young people. Co-ordinated work at local level, through Drug Action Teams, will continue.

3.15   The Home Office Drugs Prevention Initiative will disseminate widely what it learns from the continuing four year programme to evaluate a broad range of local initiatives to prevent drug misuse. These initiatives include work with parents, with community groups, with schools, with young people and with criminal justice agencies. The evaluation will look at ways of breaking the cycle of drugs and crime at an early stage and will contribute to new national guidelines for interventions in the criminal justice system, on which the Government will consult widely.

3.16   For offenders aged 16 or over, the Crime and Disorder Bill will provide a new community penalty – the drug treatment and testing order – giving courts the opportunity to monitor the progress of drug misusing offenders who are undergoing treatment as part of their sentence. Offenders who agree to undergo treatment under the order may be obliged to submit to regular testing, and will have to return to court so that the sentencers can see their progress.

4.1 To respond effectively to youth crime, we must stop making excuses for children who offend. Of course there are social, economic and family factors which affect the likelihood and the nature of youth crime. But understanding this helps us to comprehend, not to condone, youth crime. As they develop, children must bear an increasing responsibility for their actions, just as the responsibility of parents gradually declines – but does not disappear – as their children approach adulthood.

4.2 The Government is determined to reinforce the responsibility of young offenders – and their parents – for their delinquent behaviour. As a first step, section 45 of the Crime (Sentences) Act 1997 was implemented in October 1997. This extends the discretion of youth courts to allow that the names of juveniles aged 10-17 be released following conviction, where this is in the public interest. The Crime and Disorder Bill will include further important provisions to end the excuse culture, set out below.

Are children 'incapable of evil'?

4.3 Currently, for a child aged over ten but under 14 to be convicted of a criminal offence in England or Wales, the prosecution must rebut the presumption of doli incapax as well as prove the offence. This means they must prove beyond reasonable doubt that the child not only did the act in question, but that he or she knew that what they were doing was seriously wrong, rather than just naughty. To rebut the presumption, the prosecution must adduce evidence separate from the facts of the alleged offence, to show the young person knew the act in question was seriously wrong. This can lead to real practical difficulties, delaying cases or even making it impossible for the prosecution to proceed.

4.4 The Government believes that in presuming that children of this age generally do not know the difference between naughtiness and serious wrongdoing, the notion of doli incapax is contrary to common sense. The practical difficulties which the presumption presents for the prosecution can stop some children who should be prosecuted and punished for their offences from being convicted or from even coming to court. This is not in the interests of justice, of victims or of the young people themselves. If children are prosecuted where appropriate, interventions can be made to help prevent any further offending.

4.5 The consultation paper *Tackling Youth Crime* sought views on the Government's proposal to abolish – rather than reverse – the presumption of doli incapax. The Government remains of the view that abolition is necessary to remove the practical difficulties prosecutors and courts face under the current law and which they would continue to face if the presumption were reversed, rather than abolished.

Parents' responsibilities

4.6 Parents of young offenders may not directly be to blame for the crimes of their children, but parents have to be responsible for providing their children with proper care and control. The courts need powers to help and support parents more effectively to keep their children out of trouble.

4.7 Research has shown that inadequate parental supervision is strongly associated with offending – in a Home Office study, 42% of juveniles who had low or medium levels of parental supervision offended, but only 20% of juveniles with high level of supervision[2]. The same research showed that the quality of

> The presumption of doli incapax gives rise to genuine difficulties in practice. In a recent case a boy who had first been cautioned at the age of twelve embarked on a spree of offending over the next twelve months, resulting in his eventual conviction for offences including criminal damage, arson, robbery, witness intimidation, common assault, assault occasioning actual bodily harm, theft from a vehicle, theft of a vehicle and driving whilst disqualified.
>
> The prosecution of these offences was hampered by the need, in each case, to rebut the presumption of doli incapax. The boy attended a special school and the prosecution relied on the headmaster, who had known the boy for 5 years, to give evidence rebutting the presumption. Rather than allow the prosecution in subsequent cases to present this evidence in writing, the defence insisted that the headmaster be called in person in every contested case. He thus had to attend court on a number of occasions and gave evidence in at least two trials. The defence appealed against conviction, arguing among other things that the headmaster should not have been called to give evidence to rebut the presumption, because he was himself a victim of the offender. The appeal was rejected and sentence finally passed one year after the cases had first come to court.

relationship between parent and child is crucial and that poor relationships with fathers were more prevalent among offenders than poor relationships with mothers. We know that parents who are harsh or erratic in disciplining their children are twice as likely to have children who offend[13].

4.8   In the United States, a study as long ago as 1973 showed that by training parents in negotiation skills, in sticking to clear rules and rewarding good behaviour, offending rates among children were halved[14]. The Government believes that for many parents whose children get into trouble, help from trained professionals and contact with other parents in the same situation may prove invaluable. Research by organisations such as Crime Concern, the Family Policy Studies Institute and NACRO also points to the value of parenting education in helping to prevent youth criminality[15].

4.9   There are already examples in the United Kingdom of promising schemes to help and support parents in caring for and controlling their children[16]:

- Home Start, a network of nearly 200 home visiting schemes, uses trained volunteer parents to offer friendship, practical advice and support to families in difficulties;

- an experimental project sponsored by the Home Office has been run by the Dorset Healthy Alliance, promoting closer links between parents and schools to tackle problems such as truancy, bullying and disruptive behaviour. Results show some reduction in disruptive behaviour and underline the need for early intervention and support to prevent children with serious problems from becoming disruptive; and

- the Parent Network offers a 13 week course for parents which aims to improve the quality of family life and reduce the likelihood of family breakdown. An evaluation found that 70% of parents said they observed significant improvements in their children's behaviour and almost 90% said they felt better able to deal with their children's problems.

4.10   Parentline offers a helpline service for parents under stress to try to prevent child neglect and, with a recent National Lottery award, will be developing a comprehensive national information centre. In addition, the Department of Health has funded various initiatives to help children in need and their families, such as the Family Support Initiative and the Parenting Initiative. £700,000 is being spent re-focusing children's services, encouraging local authorities to shift towards preventive work to minimise the need for crisis intervention. A five year, £2.5 million project is currently running to investigate how Government support can best be mobilised to promote better parenting.

The parenting order

4.11   The Crime and Disorder Bill will establish a new **parenting order** designed to help and support parents to control the behaviour of their children. Proposals were set out in the consultation paper *Tackling Youth Crime*. The order will be available for parents of convicted young offenders, for parents of children who have been made the subject of an anti-social behaviour order, sex offender order or child safety order and for parents who have been convicted of failing to send their children to school.

4.12   The parenting order will require the parent to attend counselling or guidance sessions no more than once a week and for no longer than three months. If courts think this necessary, they may also impose additional requirements on parents – for example, seeing that their child gets to school every day, or ensuring that he or she is home by a certain time at night – which may apply for up to a year.

> **How would the parenting order work?**
>
> **Take, for example a convicted 13 year old boy who committed a number of crimes late at night and who does not attend school regularly. A parenting order might be imposed which required his parents to attend training and included additional requirements that they ensure his attendance at school and that one of them or another responsible adult be home at night to supervise him.**

Reparation

4.13   Reparation can be a valuable way of making young offenders face the consequences of their actions and see the harm they have caused. It can be a catalyst for reform and rehabilitation and can also benefit victims – who may receive compensation, an apology or the chance to ask offenders why they committed the offence and to say how it made them feel.

> **The Leeds Victim Offender Unit, started in 1985 with Home Office funding, offers victim-offender mediation, information to victims and an opportunity for victims to confront offenders and for offenders to offer reparation. The service is now offered across the whole of West Yorkshire. Internal research found that of 69 offenders involved in the scheme in 1992, 78% had no further convictions after 12 months and 58% had none after 2 years.**

4.14   **As set out in the consultation document** *Tackling Youth Crime*, the Crime and Disorder Bill will provide a new penalty – the **reparation order** – which courts will have to consider imposing on young offenders in all cases where they do not impose a compensation order. The order will require reparation to be made in kind, up to a maximum of 24 hours' work within a period of three months. The reparation might involve writing a letter of apology, apologising to the victim in person, cleaning graffiti or repairing criminal damage.

4.15   Of course, not all victims want reparation. The Government's proposals ensure that the victim's views will be sought before an order is made. Where a victim does not want direct reparation, the reparation may be made to the community at large.

4.16   Interventions following a police **Final Warning** and the **action plan order** (see chapter 5) may also include elements of reparation. And the Children and Young Persons Act 1969 will be amended so that a court may include reparation as one of the requirements of a **supervision order**. Provisions will be included in the Crime and Disorder Bill.

CHAPTER 5

EFFECTIVE INTERVENTION

IN THE COMMUNITY

5.1   Punishment is necessary to signal society's disapproval when any person – including a young person – breaks the law and as a deterrent. If the youth justice system is to fulfil its aim of preventing offending by young people, disposals should focus on changing behaviour as well as on punishment. For repeat offenders, punishments should also be progressive. Young people who ignore the help offered them, and continue to offend regardless, should be in no doubt about the tough penalties they will face – including custody if that is necessary to protect the public.

Protecting children under ten

5.2   More needs to be done to help prevent children under the age of criminal responsibility from turning to crime. What happens to children when they are very young can influence their chances of becoming offenders. Research shows that the younger the age at which children begin to 'offend' the more likely they are to continue offending[11].

5.3   We know that the quality of relationships within families and the degree of parental supervision can be crucial in predicting which children are likely to get into trouble with the law[2]. The Government proposes more support for parents facing the problems of bringing up difficult and disorderly children, through the new parenting order (see Chapter 4).

5.4   We also know that peer pressure can exert a very strong influence over children and young people: associating with delinquent peers has been shown to increase the odds of a young person offending by a factor of three[2]. New measures were set out in the consultation paper *Tackling Youth Crime* and will be included in the Crime and Disorder Bill to help young children break away from negative peer pressure and to take their lives in more positive directions.

5.5   **The child safety order** is designed to protect children under ten who are at risk of becoming involved in crime or who have already started to behave in an anti-social or criminal manner. It will be available to local authorities in the family proceedings court. Under a child safety order, a court will be able to require a child, for example, to be home at specified times or to stay away from certain people or places. The court could also prohibit certain conduct, such as truanting from school. A child safety order could be linked with a parenting order if the court felt that to be appropriate. If the requirements of an order are not complied with, it will be open to the local authority to commence care proceedings under Section 31(1)(a) of the Children Act 1989.

How would the child safety order work?

For example, an 8 year old girl found shoplifting with a group of older girls in the local shopping centre might be referred by the police to social services. The local authority could apply to the court for a child safety order. The order might require her to stay away from the shopping centre, not mix with the older girls and (with the agreement of the organisers) attend a local youth programme to make constructive use of her leisure time.

5.6 Local child curfew – for their own good, and to prevent neighbourhood crime or disorder, young children should not be out, unsupervised late at night. The Crime and Disorder Bill will provide new powers for local authorities and the police to set up curfew schemes for children under ten. Before establishing a scheme, a local authority would have to consult the police and the local community and obtain approval from the Home Secretary. The council may then bar children under ten from specified public areas after a specified time (which would not be earlier than 9.00 pm) unless they are accompanied by a responsible person. Local curfews established under an approved scheme may only last for up to 90 days. If the local authority seeks an extension beyond this, it will have to consult again with the police and local community.

5.7 A child under ten who is found out unaccompanied in a curfew area during curfew hours may be taken home by the police into the care of a responsible person. If there is no responsible person there to look after him or her, the police might use powers already available to them under section 46 of the Children Act 1989 to remove the child to other suitable accommodation.

5.8 Curfew schemes should provide an effective immediate method of dealing with clearly identified problems of anti-social and disorderly children who are too young to be left out unsupervised late at night. Schemes should be integrated into the area's wider community safety strategy.

> **How would a local child curfew work? For example, if young children were regularly congregating at night in the public spaces of a housing estate, making residents' lives intolerable through vandalism, pilfering and abusive behaviour, local residents might seek the help of the police. If normal policing methods did not work the local authority and police, after consultation, might decide to introduce a local child curfew for a ninety day period.**

Before a young offender gets to court – nipping offending in the bud

5.9 The great majority of young offenders commit offences only once or twice. In these cases, a warning by the police is often the most effective way of preventing further crime. Around 68% of offenders who are cautioned for the first time are not cautioned again or reconvicted within two years[7]. However, cautions grow progressively less effective as they are repeated. The Audit Commission in 1996 pointed to evidence suggesting that after three occasions, prosecution is more effective than cautioning in preventing re-offending[3].

5.10 The trouble with the current cautioning system is that it is too haphazard and that too often a caution does not result in any follow up action, so the opportunity is lost for early intervention to turn youngsters away from crime. While some areas operate voluntary 'caution-plus' schemes, in others there is no backup to try to prevent further crime. Inconsistent, repeated and ineffective cautioning has allowed some children and young people to feel that they can offend with impunity.

5.11 The previous Government attempted to impose greater rigour and consistency in the use of police cautions. Guidelines issued in 1994 discouraged the use of second cautions except where the second offence was trivial or there had been a long gap since the first offence. Following this guidance there was evidence of a reduction in repeat cautioning, but no evidence that the 1994 circular and its predecessors had been successful in achieving greater consistency in practice between forces[17]. The Government believes that more radical action is now needed.

The Final Warning

5.12 The Crime and Disorder Bill will abolish cautioning for young offenders and replace it with a statutory police reprimand and Final Warning scheme. Within a clear statutory framework, the police will decide whether to reprimand a young offender, give a Final Warning, or bring criminal charges. When a Final Warning is given, this will usually be followed by a community intervention programme, involving the offender and his or her family to address the causes of the offending and so reduce the risk of further crime. The police officer issuing the Final Warning will explain to the young person how the Final Warning intervention will work.

5.13   The consultation paper *Tackling Youth Crime* explained the scheme:

- a first offence might be met by a police reprimand, provided it was not serious. Any further offence would have to result in a Final Warning or criminal charges: in no circumstances should a young offender receive two reprimands;

- if a first offence results in a Final Warning, any further offence would automatically lead to criminal charges, except where at least two years have passed since the Final Warning and the subsequent offence is minor; and

- for any offence the police would have the option of pressing charges.

5.14   The consultation paper *Tackling Youth Crime* also proposed that any 10-19 year old convicted of a further offence within two years of receiving a Final Warning should not be able to receive a conditional discharge when sentenced for the subsequent offence. In the light of consultation responses, the Government has decided to allow courts discretion, in exceptional circumstances, to use a conditional discharge in such cases.

5.15   The Final Warning scheme will ensure that more consistent action is taken, before a young offender ever appears in court, to try to nip offending in the bud. Where a young person nevertheless continues to offend, court action will be necessary.

Caution-plus schemes are already running successfully in a number of areas. Final Warning interventions could build on programmes such as:

Thames Valley's scheme in Aylesbury which works with young offenders who agree to co-operate rather than face charges. If the victim agrees, an offender will apologise face to face, and hear from the victim about the effects of the crime. The programme is demanding for offenders and both victims and young offenders have found it worthwhile. More detailed research will be conducted, but Thames Valley's initial findings in terms of re-offending rates among young offenders who have participated in the project are promising.

The **Northamptonshire Diversion Unit**: intervention packages are prepared following consultation with the offender and the victim(s) and tailored to the individual offender to address the offence and prevent re-offending. For example, a teenage boy who had caused damage to a church agreed to a package which included apologising to the church warden, gardening work in the church grounds and paying a contribution towards the cost of repairing the damage.

Both offenders and victims have benefited – the Diversion Unit reports that only 3% of offenders decline to co-operate; and 76% of victims are satisfied with the way the offences are resolved. Research conducted by Nene College estimated that the Unit's results were "consistent with the view that the Diversion Unit has played a significant role in reducing re-offending". The Unit estimates that the cost of a caution and referral to the Unit is less than 25% of the cost of disposal by prosecution.

Widening the range of effective community penalties

5.16   The Government will extend the range of community penalties for young offenders. Provisions in the Crime (Sentences) Act 1997 allowing courts to impose curfew orders with electronic tagging on 10-15 year old offenders will be implemented on a pilot basis, starting in Norfolk and Greater Manchester in January 1998. The pilots will be carefully evaluated.

5.17   Already, the indications from existing schemes testing tagging on adults are that a curfew order backed by electronic monitoring can help offenders to structure their lives better, and help ensure compliance with other community penalties[18].

More effective community penalties

5.18   The Crime and Disorder Bill will include a new kind of community penalty for young offenders – the **action plan order** – a short, intensive programme of community intervention combining punishment, rehabilitation and reparation to change offending behaviour and prevent further crime.

5.19   Proposals were set out in the consultation paper *Tackling Youth Crime*. The order will be available for 10 -17 year old and will impose requirements designed to address the specific causes of offending. Each order will last for three months.

5.20   The consultation paper *Tackling Youth Crime* also included proposals to make the existing **supervision order** more effective. Amendments to the Children and Young Persons Act 1969 will enable courts to impose residency requirements on any young person who breaches, or who offends during the course of, a supervision order, if their living arrangements contributed to a significant extent to that breach or offence. Breach arrangements for supervision orders will also be simplified.

How would the action plan order work?

Before imposing an action plan order, a court would consider a written report from the local Youth Offending Team, drawn up following consultation with the young offender, his or her family, and perhaps also the victim. The report would specify the requirements which the YOT proposed for an action plan.

The plan will be tailored to the individual young offender, targeting offending behaviour and aimed at preventing further offending. It may include elements such as motor projects, anger management courses, alcohol or drug treatment programmes or help with problems at home or at school or in finding accommodation, training or employment.

CHAPTER 6

EFFECTIVE CUSTODIAL

PENALTIES AND REMANDS

6.1   Preceding chapters have focused on community interventions, both before and after a young person reaches court, to protect the public by preventing offending and re-offending. For the most serious and persistent young offenders, courts must also have the option of sentencing – and remanding – to custody.

What is wrong with current provision?

6.2   The present custodial arrangements for 10 –17 year olds are widely viewed as unsatisfactory:

- the available accommodation is fragmented and regimes vary both in quality and cost;

- courts' powers to remand young people to secure facilities are inadequate and inappropriate;

- the sentencing framework can lead to arbitrary outcomes: the kind of institution in which the sentence is served is to a large extent determined by the powers under which the young person is sentenced rather than the needs of the young person; and

- the structure of sentences does not allow for sufficient emphasis to be placed on preventing offending or responding to progress.

This chapter sets out how the Government intends to reform these chaotic and dysfunctional arrangements.

Review of secure accommodation

6.3   The Government has instituted a review of the whole range of secure accommodation for young offenders and young people held on remand[19]. The review is examining how to make better use of existing and planned accommodation to ensure that provision is more consistent and coherent and that regimes tackle criminality and meet the educational and other needs of these young people. It is being conducted by the Home Office in collaboration with the Department of Health, the Welsh Office and the Treasury and involving local authorities. The review covers local authority secure units; Prison Service accommodation, including Young Offender Institutions; Secure Training Centres; and the Department of Health Youth Treatment Centre and will be completed shortly.

6.4   Powers in the Crime and Disorder Bill will enable the new Youth Justice Board for England and Wales (see chapter 8) to act as budget-holder and commissioner of all secure facilities for young offenders, if this is considered appropriate in the light of the review. In addition, the Youth Justice Board will help set and monitor standards for secure accommodation.

Regimes for young offenders

6.5   A significant programme of work is also underway to review and improve arrangements and regimes for holding young offenders in the penal system. The Government believes that a custodial sentence should not be an end in itself – it protects the public by removing the young offender from the opportunity to offend, but the fundamental aim of both custodial and community sentences, in line with the aim of the youth justice system, should be to prevent offending. The Government wants to see constructive regimes, including education and a high standard of care, to help give young offenders a better chance of staying out of trouble once released.

Remands to secure accommodation

6.6   The Government believes that the courts should have clear powers to remand to secure accommodation, young people aged 10-16 who are awaiting trial, where this is necessary to protect the public. At present, courts may remand juveniles to local authority accommodation but are not able to specify that they be kept in secure local authority accommodation (though the local authority may apply to the court for the young person to be held in secure accommodation). Currently courts may only order a secure remand for 15 and 16 year old boys and only to Prison Service accommodation.

6.7   The Criminal Justice Act 1991 and the Criminal Justice and Public Order Act 1994 contain provisions to amend the Children and Young Persons Act 1969 to allow courts to remand 12-16 year olds directly to secure local authority accommodation when certain conditions are met. These provisions, however, have not been implemented. The previous Government began a building programme to provide 170 new local authority secure places which will be completed in 1998. The additional places will not be sufficient to meet the full likely demand for remand places for 12 -16 year olds. The Government proposes to use the Crime and Disorder Bill to enable implementation of court ordered secure remand powers for certain groups of young people. Its priorities are to:

- introduce court-ordered remands direct to local authority secure accommodation for all 12-14 year olds and for 15 and 16 year old girls as soon as practicable; and

- enable the most vulnerable 15 and 16 year old boys to be remanded by the courts direct to local authority secure accommodation, rather than prison, if a place has been identified.

The legislation will specify that vulnerable boys are those whom a court considers should not be remanded to prison because of their physical or emotional immaturity or their propensity to harm themselves. Other 15 and 16 year old boys, for the meantime, will continue to be remanded to Prison Service accommodation. Regime standards currently being developed by the Prison Service will include provisions to safeguard the welfare of young people, consistent with the need to protect the public and staff.

6.8   The Government believes that this approach will ensure that the courts have the powers that they need to protect the public, and the young person, from offending while awaiting trial. It will also help protect the welfare of young people by providing some flexibility over where 15 and 16 year old boys are held.

A new custodial sentence

6.9   Existing legislation provides for a number of different custodial penalties for 10-17 year olds:

- detention at Her Majesty's pleasure, under section 53(1) of the Children and Young Persons Act 1933 for murder: the sentence may be served in local authority secure accommodation or Prison Service accommodation depending on the age and vulnerability of the offender and the availability of accommodation;

- long terms of detention, under section 53(2) of the 1933 Act, up to the adult maximum, for other very serious offences such as manslaughter, robbery, domestic burglary and indecent assault: the sentence may be served in local authority secure accommodation or Prison Service accommodation depending on the offender's age and vulnerability and the availability of accommodation;

- detention of between 2 months and 2 years in a Young Offender Institution for 15 - 17 year olds convicted of any imprisonable offence; and

- a secure training order of between 6 months and 2 years for 12–14 year old persistent offenders to be served in secure training centres (the relevant provisions of the 1994 Criminal Justice and Public Order Act are to be brought into force in 1998).

6.10   The use of custody is subject to the sentencing framework set out in the Criminal Justice Act 1991. This provides that custody may be imposed only where the offence (or it and associated offences) is so serious that only custody can be justified or, if it is a sexual or violent offence, where only custody would be adequate to protect the public from serious harm.

6.11   The Government does not propose to move away from the principles set out in the 1991 Act and also believes that the courts should retain powers to impose section 53 sentences equivalent to adult penalties on the most serious young offenders. It proposes, however, to replace the sentences of detention in a Young Offender Institution and the secure training order with a more constructive and flexible custodial sentence providing a clear focus on preventing offending. The aim is to ensure that custodial sentences, where they are necessary, are more effective in preventing further crime. The Government has drawn on advice from the Youth Justice Task Force in preparing a new regime of **detention and training orders**.

A new generic sentence – the detention and training order

6.12   The Government will introduce a new disposal available for 10–17 year olds, the detention and training order (DTO). It will be subject to the restrictions on use of custody laid down in the 1991 Criminal Justice Act, i.e. courts may impose the order only where the offence or offences in question are so serious that only custody is justified. For 10 and 11 year olds, the power to make an order would be available only in response to persistent offending and only where the court

considers that a custodial sentence is necessary to protect the public from further offending by that child. For 12–14 year olds, the DTO could be imposed only in relation to persistent offending. For 15–17 year olds, it would be available for any imprisonable offence sufficiently serious to justify custody under the 1991 Act.

6.13   In the first instance, the Government will implement the order only for 12–17 year olds. But there will be a discretionary power for the Home Secretary to introduce the DTO for 10 and 11 year olds, by order laid before Parliament, if this proves necessary or desirable at a later date.

6.14   Half the length of the DTO will be spent in custody and half under community supervision, with provision for shortening or extending the custodial element depending on the young offender's progress against an agreed sentence plan. Orders will range in length from a minimum of four months to a maximum of two years with orders of 6, 8, 10, 12 and 18 months available. Courts will be required to take account of remand time as well as the seriousness of the offending in deciding the length of sentence instead of time spent in custody on remand being deducted after sentence from the time to be served in custody.

Recognising good progress

6.15   In order to respond to good or bad progress, for longer sentences there will be some flexibility in release date. For DTOs lasting between a total of 8–12 months, a young person making good progress against his or her sentence plan might be released from custody a month before the half-way point. For longer sentences, one or two months' early release would be available. Conversely, if poor progress were made, with the agreement of the court, a young offender sentenced to an order lasting 8–12 months could be held in custody for a month beyond the 50% point and one sentenced to 18 or 24 months could be held for one or two months beyond the normal release date.

6.16   For DTOs lasting less than 8 months, there would be no specific arrangement for early release to reflect good progress, but the general arrangements in the Crime and Disorder Bill for home detention curfews – as announced by the Home Secretary on 20 November 1997 – would apply. Implementation of the home curfew arrangements for juveniles will be subject to the successful completion of pilot studies of the related curfew order for 10-15 year olds, due to start in January 1998.

Supervision after release from custody

6.17   A supervising officer - a member of the Youth Offending Team (see chapter 8) – would be appointed at the start of the sentence. He or she would be responsible for supervision after release from custody and would also be involved in the planning and supervision of the custodial element. Whether the young offender was released from custody early, late or at the normal half-way point, the period of supervision would last until the end of the sentence. A young offender who breached his or her supervision requirements during the normal supervision period would be liable to a fine of up to level three (currently £1,000) or to be returned to custody for three months or the remainder of the sentence, whichever is the shorter.

Where would young offenders sentenced to DTOs be detained?

6.18   The order will be served in any accommodation deemed to be suitable by the Home Secretary. This could mean a Young Offender Institution, a secure training centre, Youth Treatment Centre or local authority secure unit. How this works in practice will need to take account of the outcome of the review of the secure estate (see paragraph 6.3). The Youth Justice Board will set and monitor standards to ensure high quality and consistent regimes.

6.19   Under the new arrangements, therefore, there will be scope for individual young offenders to be placed in secure accommodation depending on their age and maturity. The new arrangements will allow the Home Secretary to delegate the responsibility for placements to local Youth Offending Teams, rather than having placements decided centrally.

6.20   The Government believes the new detention and training order will provide clearer, simpler, more flexible and more consistent custodial arrangements for young offenders. The increased emphasis on supervision after release, on a clear sentence plan to tackle the causes of offending and on continuity of supervision before and after release from custody should provide for a more effective custodial sentence, complementing the Government's proposals for more effective community penalties.

How long does it take before a young offender is sentenced?

7.1   In 1996, it took an average of 131 days (about four and a half months) to deal with a young offender from arrest to sentence[20]. The Audit Commission in its study *Misspent Youth* found that 4 out of 5 cases observed were adjourned at least once and that, on average, each young offender appeared in court four times during the progress of his or her case[3].

7.2   The Government is particularly concerned by delays in dealing with persistent young offenders. In 1996 it took an average of 142 days between arrest and sentence for persistent young offenders.

7.3   The Government is determined to end these delays. They impede justice, frustrate victims and bring the law into disrepute. And delays do no favours to young offenders themselves: they increase the risk of offending on bail and they postpone intervention to address offending behaviour. The top priority will be to halve the time taken between arrest and sentence for persistent young offenders, by fast-tracking them through the system.

How can delays be reduced?

7.4   Many youth justice practitioners are already making efforts to tackle delay, with Government encouragement. The Lord Chancellor wrote to chairmen of youth court panels in May 1997 and a circular issued in October set out good practice and asked local agencies to set up fast-track schemes for persistent young offenders[21]. The Government plans to contact youth justice practitioners in spring 1998 to find out what action has been taken to give effect to the circular's recommendations and in particular to establish fast-tracking schemes.

7.5   Research undertaken by the Audit Commission in the first four months of 1997 shows that the time taken to deal with young offenders varies enormously from area to area. In some areas, it took up to 220 days or more than 7 months on average between arrest and sentence. In Gwynedd, the area with the best performance, average periods between arrest and sentence were only 81 days. The Government wants to see all areas emulate the practice of the best.

Crime and Disorder Bill

7.6   A good deal can be achieved within the existing statutory framework. But to implement the pledge to halve the time taken to sentence persistent young offenders, and to ensure permanent improvements right across England and Wales, legislative changes are necessary. The Government set out its proposals in the consultation paper *Tackling Delays in the Youth Justice System* and these will be taken forward through the Crime and Disorder Bill.

> **In some areas, agencies are already working together to reduce delays.**
>
> **For example, Middlesbrough has achieved an average of 83 days or 12 weeks between arrest and sentence. The police use gravity factors to help them decide in the majority of cases on the day of arrest whether to caution or charge; no cases are referred to a multi-agency panel. Where the police decide to prosecute, most cases are prepared within two weeks where a**

guilty plea is anticipated, and three weeks where the charge is contested. Teesside Magistrates' Court runs a youth court user group which meets regularly to deal with problems.

In North Hampshire, the fast-tracking scheme involves all local youth justice agencies. An information booklet explaining what to do before coming to court is given to young offenders; advance disclosure of the prosecution case is prepared and dispatched to the young offender's home (unless the CPS is notified of legal representation) at least 7 days in advance of first hearing; legal aid applications are generally determined and notified to the solicitors within 48 hours of receipt; all young offenders are charged and bailed, rather than summonsed, to a first hearing in 28 days; first hearing dates are fixed by direct telephone line between the charge centre and court scheduling department; and to avoid adjournments for the preparation of new pre-sentence reports, the Youth Justice Service provides verbal updates to existing PSRs .

The average time between charge and first appearance has been reduced from 69 days to 44; and the average time between charge and sentence has been brought down from 133 days to 89.

7.7   **Review of Delay in the Criminal Justice System** – the Government will be implementing most of the recommendations of this review[22], some of them through the Crime and Disorder Bill. Many should significantly speed up juvenile justice, including measures to:

- enable cases in which a straightforward guilty plea is expected to be heard within a few days of charge;

- promote the effective management of the pre-trial preparation of cases: the Crime and Disorder Bill will make provision for certain powers to be exercised by a single justice, and for these powers to be delegated where appropriate to justices' clerks. The Government is giving further consideration to which of the powers could properly be delegated to justices' clerks; and

- to allow the youth court, when dealing with a young person charged with a grave offence which is committed to the Crown Court, to commit related offences as well, so that all can be proceeded with together.

7.8   **Reversing R v Khan** – this 1994 ruling has led to unwelcome delays in the youth court. The Crime and Disorder Bill will ensure that where a youth court commits a case to the Crown Court it need not await the outcome of the Crown Court trial before sentencing the same defendant on unrelated charges.

7.9   The Crime and Disorder Bill will also clarify that where the youth court is dealing with offenders who face multiple charges (including so called 'spree' offenders), they do not have to adjourn in order to tie up all outstanding charges.

7.10   **Statutory time limits** – the measures in paragraphs 7.7, 7.8 and 7.9, together with the adoption of best practice, will create the conditions in which delays should be reduced significantly. To ensure that performance measures up, the Government will set mandatory time limits covering all criminal proceedings involving young people, using powers under the Prosecution of Offences Act 1985, as modified and extended by the Crime and Disorder Bill.

7.11   Time limits for cases involving young people will be stricter than for those involving adults and tougher limits still will be set for cases involving persistent young offenders.

7.12 Time limits will cover most of the period from arrest to sentence. The period of the trial itself will not be covered by a time limit, as this would risk undermining the fairness of the court proceedings (and, in the vast majority of cases, the trial period does not contribute significantly to delay). In guilty plea cases, there would be no interval between start of trial and conviction. The time limits would in effect run through from arrest to sentence without a gap.

7.13 The length of the time limits themselves will be set following consultation and following pilot trials. Time limits will be implemented only once the new streamlined procedures set out in paragraphs 7.7 – 7.9 are in place.

7.14 **Enforcing statutory time limits –** The Government will introduce tighter criteria for granting extensions to time limits and provide for a new, more flexible, sanction when the prosecution exceeds one of the new time limits. At the moment, if the prosecution overruns a time limit, they are 'punished' by the defendant effectively being acquitted. The Government proposes instead that where the prosecution fails to meet a time limit, the charge should automatically be 'set aside', allowing the prosecution to recommence at a later date if the Director of Public Prosecutions or a Chief Crown Prosecutor thinks it appropriate.

7.15 In addition to the sanctions outlined above, the Government is considering whether fixed penalty style sanctions may be practicable for defence solicitors who fail to meet a deadline set by the court. The courts will also be able to enforce statutory time limits by making use of their existing power, to impose 'wasted costs orders', which are applicable to both prosecution and defence.

7.16 **Performance targets** – experience with existing non-statutory time guidelines (set by the inter-Departmental Trials Issues Group) has shown that upper limits can come to be seen as targets. That is why, in addition to statutory time limits (which are upper limits) the Government also proposes to introduce more demanding, non-statutory, performance targets. Performance against these targets will be monitored by the new Youth Justice Board (see chapter 8). The Board may publish the information it obtains, so giving greater accountability and a strong incentive to improved performance. The Home Secretary will, at the request of the Board, consult the Lord Chancellor and the Attorney General on the provision to, and publication by, the Board of information on the operation of the courts or the Crown Prosecution Service.

7.17 **Fast-tracking persistent young offenders** – To help deliver the key pledge to halve the time it takes to get persistent young offenders from arrest to sentence, statutory time limits for persistent young offenders will be the most demanding. A "persistent young offender" will be defined as someone aged 10-17 who has been sentenced for one or more recordable offences on three or more separate occasions and is arrested again (or has an information laid against him or her) within three years of last being sentenced. In practice, the Government would expect others who do not fit this exact profile – in particular 'spree offenders' who commit multiple offences over a short period – to be fast-tracked so that if they are found guilty, their offending may be addressed quickly.

CHAPTER 8

NATIONAL LEADERSHIP,

LOCAL PARTNERSHIP

8.1   The youth justice system should protect the public by preventing offending by young people. The preceding chapters have set out plans for new methods of intervention before and after young people get to court to deliver that aim. This chapter explains the new structures the Government will put in place to deliver youth justice services more effectively. These measures were published for consultation in the document *New National and Local Focus on Youth Crime.*

A new national framework

8.2   For too long there has been a lack of clear direction in the youth justice system. The Government will give the necessary leadership - setting out clearly in legislation the aim of the youth justice system and establishing a national body to monitor the delivery of youth justice services and help to raise standards.

8.3   The Crime and Disorder Bill will establish a **Youth Justice Board** for England and Wales, as a Non-Departmental Public Body sponsored by the Home Office. Its functions will be to:

- monitor the operation and performance of the youth justice system, including the youth court, the work of Youth Offending Teams and the delivery of secure accommodation. The Board will report to the Home Secretary as appropriate, who will refer issues relating to the courts to the Lord Chancellor;

- advise the Home Secretary on drawing up standards for the work of Youth Offending Teams and the juvenile secure estate, monitor performance against those standards and publish results;

- identify and disseminate good practice, including commissioning research and providing financial assistance for developing new approaches; and

- advise the Home Secretary on the operation of the youth justice system in delivering its aim and changes which may be needed.

8.4   The Crime and Disorder Bill will also allow for the Youth Justice Board to become the commissioning and purchasing body for secure facilities for young offenders if, following the review of secure accommodation, this is considered appropriate (see paragraph 6.4).

8.5   By monitoring and, where appropriate, publishing information on performance across the youth justice systems, the Youth Justice Board will encourage greater accountability and openness. Many of those who work in the youth justice system are public servants and the public deserve to know that the youth justice system is working effectively on their behalf.

8.6   The Board will be accountable to the Home Secretary for the performance of its functions. The Home Secretary will, in turn, be accountable to Parliament for the decisions he takes on the advice of the Youth Justice Board; for the efficiency and effectiveness of the Board, and its usefulness; and for the public money it spends.

New local partnerships

8.7   The consultation document *New National and Local Focus on Youth Crime* also set out proposals for a network of local inter-agency teams to deliver a range of youth justice services to the courts and the community. Young offenders often present multiple problems - for example, drug or alcohol misuse, problems at school or problems at home. It makes sense for the agencies which deal with each of these issues to come together locally, to address these problems and so reduce the risk of further crime.

8.8 The Crime and Disorder Bill will place a duty on local authorities with social services and education responsibilities to ensure the provision of a **Youth Offending Team(s)** (YOT(s)) in their area, in partnership with the other relevant local agencies. The other key agencies - the probation committee and the police and health authorities - will be under a reciprocal duty to participate in YOTs, in accordance with guidance to be issued by the Government. YOTs will also need to work with agencies such as the courts and the Prison Service and alongside complementary inter-agency groups such as the new community safety and crime reduction partnerships to be established under the Crime and Disorder Bill, and local Drug Reference Groups, many of which have been established at the district level. In some cases, local arrangements of this kind are already in place. The Government is determined to see greater consistency across the whole of England and Wales.

8.9 At the operational level, YOTs will include social workers, probation officers, police officers and education and health authority staff. They might also include people from other agencies and organisations, including those in the voluntary sector. The most important requirement is that YOTs should have the right blend of skills and experience and that all team members should have a common approach to youth justice, focused on addressing offending behaviour.

8.10 YOTs' functions will include:

- assessment and intervention work in support of the Final Warning;

- supervision of community punishments for young offenders;

- provision of "appropriate adult" services, bail information, bail supervision and support;

- placement of young people on remand in open or secure accommodation;

- court work and the preparation of reports;

- throughcare and supervision of youngsters who have been released from custody; and

- preventative work taking account of the work of local authority youth services (including, where appropriate, supervising parenting and child safety orders).

8.11 As set out in paragraph 6.19, the Home Secretary will be enabled, under the Crime and Disorder Bill, to delegate to YOTs the responsibility for placing young offenders in secure accommodation.

8.12 The Government remains of the view that it would be best to leave the appointment of managers of YOTs to local decision on the basis of merit, rather than prescribe that managers should come from one specific agency. However, the Task Force on Youth Justice has been asked to undertake further work on YOTs to ensure proper accountability for their work.

YOT interventions

8.13 YOTs will bring together the experience and skills of relevant local agencies to address the causes of a young person's offending - whether that may be difficulties at home or school, peer group pressure, behavioural difficulties, mental health problems or drug or alcohol misuse - and so reduce the risk of re-offending.

8.14 YOTs will deliver community intervention programmes to make youngsters face up to the consequences of their crimes and learn to change the habits and attitudes which lead them into offending and anti-social behaviour. The programmes might adopt techniques such as:

- group work;

- one to one work;

- family group conferencing; and

- mentoring.

Consistent delivery of youth justice services

8.15   The Crime and Disorder Bill will place a duty on local authorities with social services and education responsibilities to ensure that appropriate youth justice services, including appropriate bail supervision and support, are available in their area, in partnership with the other relevant local agencies. Local authorities will be required to prepare a youth justice plan setting out how the services are to be provided and funded. The probation committee and the police and health authorities will be placed under a duty to co-operate in the provision of local youth justice services in accordance with guidance issued by the Government.

Bail supervision and support

8.16   Having appropriate bail supervision and support available can help to cut costs and cut crime. Bail supervision and support can help young people to return to court when they are due - so reducing delays due to the non-appearance of defendants - and help reduce offending on bail and prevent interference with, and intimidation of, witnesses. It can also reduce the need to use secure accommodation and provide an opportunity to help young people tackle difficulties which may contribute to offending.

Mentoring

A relationship with an adult who offers experience, practical advice and a positive role model can help troubled youngsters to develop self-respect and respect for others, and a sense of personal and social responsibility. Organisations such as DIVERT Trust are developing mentoring projects.

Among promising schemes included in a Home Office study published in 1996[15] were:

- **the Dalston Youth Project in Hackney which began working with 15-19 year olds and has more recently developed a programme with 11 to 15 year olds. This is being funded, and will be evaluated, by the Home Office;**

- **the Milton Keynes Young People's Befriender Scheme, which puts young people who have been in trouble in touch with trained mentors. Informal results suggest that 80% of those involved in the scheme have not re-offended within one year; and**

- **the CHANCE Project in Islington, which includes mentoring for 5 to 10 year olds who are thought to be at risk, and which is to be evaluated by the Home Office.**

CHAPTER 9

REFORM OF THE YOUTH COURT

9.1 Underpinning the Government's reform programme is the belief that the right intervention at the right time can be highly effective at cutting short the criminal activities of young people. Previous chapters have highlighted plans for early intervention before a child or young person comes to court, for a range of new sentencing options to make young offenders take responsibility - and make amends - for their behaviour and for speeding up the youth justice system, including through better case management. But this is not enough. The Government has also been looking carefully at the way the youth court in England and Wales carries out its business, at the philosophy which underlies its proceedings and at the culture in which it operates.

A youth court for the 21st century

9.2 A frank assessment of the current approach of the youth court must conclude that, all too often, inadequate attention is given to changing offending behaviour. This is not the fault of individuals working within the system. It is encouraged by the court's very structures and procedures. The Government is determined to tackle these failings head on. The purpose of the youth court must change from simply deciding guilt or innocence and then issuing a sentence. In most cases, an offence should trigger a wider enquiry into the circumstances and nature of the offending behaviour, leading to action to change that behaviour. This requires in turn a fundamental change of approach within the youth court system.

9.3 So reform of the youth court is needed to provide:

- speedier decisions on guilt or innocence, much closer to the date of

the offence and with less tolerance of adjournments;

- a system which is more open, and which commands the confidence of victims and the public;

- processes which engage young offenders and their parents and focus on the nature of their offending behaviour and how to change it;

- a stronger emphasis on using sentencing to prevent future offending; and

- more efficient arrangements for the scheduling and management of cases.

9.4 Many of the measures described in earlier chapters will contribute to meeting these objectives, by involving young offenders and their families in preventing offending, improving the effectiveness and efficiency of present arrangements, and introducing greater openness. However, more is needed.

9.5 The Government's proposals for immediate action are outlined below, in paragraphs 9.6-9.16. Longer term reform proposals are at paragraphs 9.20-9.38.

Engaging with the offender

9.6 It is vital, when a young offender goes to the youth court, that the process involves the young person and his or her parents directly. The Government therefore plans to:

- encourage **training for magistrates** to emphasise the value of talking directly to both the young defendant and his or her parents during court proceedings, even where the young person has legal representation;

- remove any obstacles in the **Magistrates' Courts Rules,** which may prevent or discourage magistrates from questioning defendants about the reasons for their behaviour, before reaching a final decision on sentencing; and

- encourage youth courts to consider changing the **physical environment** of the court room to promote proceedings which involve the young person directly and are less adversarial. This might involve (except where the security constraints were overriding) all participants in the case, including the magistrates, sitting around a single table.

Opening up the youth court

9.7   There must also be more openness in youth court proceedings. In law, youth courts have some discretion over who can attend proceedings and over the lifting of reporting restrictions. But present practice places too much emphasis on protecting the identity of young offenders at the expense of the interests of victims and the community. Justice is best served in an open court where the criminal process can be scrutinised and the offender cannot hide behind a cloak of anonymity.

9.8   The Government believes that the youth court should make full use of its discretion to lift reporting restrictions in the public interest following conviction. This is particularly important where the offence is a serious one; where the offending is persistent or where it has affected a number of people or the local community; and at the upper age range of the youth court. Occasions when it would not be in the best interests of the public, and others concerned with the case, to lift reporting restrictions might include cases where an early guilty plea was entered or where naming the young offender would result in revealing the identity of a vulnerable victim.

9.9   Though the Government does not want to make youth courts entirely open in the same way as adult courts, it believes that magistrates should make use of their existing discretion to admit victims and members of the public to youth courts. Victims, in particular, have a strong claim to be present during the trial to see justice being done, unless in the circumstances of the particular case this would be contrary to the interests of justice.

9.10   The Government intends to issue guidance on the approach which it believes should be taken in this area.

Defence services

9.11   Anyone who is a suspect or defendant in the criminal justice process must be treated fairly, whatever their age. For this reason our system gives a number of guarantees designed to protect individuals. Some of these basic rights involve legal assistance. Under our system, people who are being questioned by the police are entitled to legal advice in private. And our practice is consistent with Article 6(3)(c) of the European Convention on Human Rights, which provides that everyone charged with a criminal offence has the right to defend himself in person, or through legal assistance of his choosing or, if he has not sufficient means to pay for legal assistance, to be given it free when the interests of justice so require.

9.12   Publicly funded defence services are provided to protect the interests of young suspects and defendants. Legal aid pays for a lawyer's help when a young person is being questioned by the police, or on many occasions when a defendant has to make up his or her mind about whether to plead guilty, in the light of the prosecution's case. The State pay for lawyers to represent defendants at trials or sentencing hearings where it is in the interests of justice: for instance, when a defendant is at risk of a custodial sentence, or where, even if there is no such risk, there are substantial issues of law to be decided.

9.13   A suspect or defendant must have a choice of lawyer. But it would be wrong for any solicitor, regardless of his or her abilities, to be able to act for a young person on legal aid. Choice should be limited to those who will advise and represent their clients robustly and who have shown that they possess the necessary skills and attributes to protect their clients' interests.

9.14   If a young person does not have his or her own lawyer and needs one, a duty solicitor will be available at the court or police station.

9.15   At present, payment to lawyers is on a time basis. This can provide a perverse incentive and encourages delay. It can result in lawyers advising clients who do not have a defence to plead guilty late rather than early or to seek unnecessary adjournments. Because of this the present payment system runs counter to the objectives of reaching speedier decisions, of making the system credible and of increasing the efficiency of case management.

9.16   The Government believes that the way to get the right kind of legal services in the youth court is through fixed price contracting as far as possible. This will ensure flexibility, quality and provide a block funded payment system rather than one in which lawyers are paid case by case. The Legal Aid Board is currently planning pilots of quality assured contracts for some criminal defence services. Pilots will begin in February 1998. Pilots for representation in youth court work would take some time to devise. It would be possible to offer solicitors the opportunity to include this work in their contracts six to nine months after the pilots start.

9.17   Extending these arrangements to cover representation in the youth court will:

- enable young suspects and defendants to have a choice of lawyer who will advise and represent them well; and

- make it possible for lawyers to be paid in ways which do not encourage delay.

9.18   The conditions for winning a contract will be designed so as to promote the

Government's objectives for youth justice. For instance, contracts could require youth court lawyers to have attended training on how to avoid formal and over-adversarial approaches and to have systems to ensure that cases can be handled quickly. Feedback on the performance of contracted lawyers might be given by the court to the Legal Aid Board.

Means testing

9.19   At present, before a defendant can be granted legal aid, his or her means, or those of his or her parents or guardians, must be tested. Depending on the outcome of the test, they may have to pay a contribution. The process involves inquiring whether what the applicant, parents or guardians say about their savings and income is correct. This takes time and resources. The Government will investigate whether means testing is justified in the youth court by the amount recovered in contributions and by the number of defendants choosing not to accept legal aid after they have been means tested. If the Government finds that means testing is cost-effective, it will consider moving the test to a later stage in the case, to reduce delays. This analysis will be completed by summer 1998.

A step change in the culture of the youth court

9.20   Taken together, the changes set out in paragraphs 9.6 – 9.19 represent a significant advance over the current operation of the youth court. But more radical action is needed to maximise the impact of the youth court on young offenders, making it as effective as possible at tackling offending behaviour, especially for young people appearing before the court for the first time.

9.21   The Government considers that it will be necessary to reshape the criminal justice system in England and Wales to produce more constructive outcomes with young offenders. Its proposals for reform build on principles underlying the concept of restorative justice:

- **restoration:** young offenders apologising to their victims and making amends for the harm they have done;

- **reintegration:** young offenders paying their debt to society, putting their crime behind them and rejoining the law abiding community; and

- **responsibility:** young offenders – and their parents – facing the consequences of their offending behaviour and taking responsibility for preventing further offending.

9.22   The new approach is intended to:

- ensure that the most serious offenders continue to be dealt with in a criminal court to provide punishment, protect the public and prevent re-offending;

- provide an opportunity for less serious offending to be dealt with in a new non-criminal panel, enforced by a criminal court;

- involve young people more effectively in decisions about them – encouraging them to admit their guilt and face up to the consequences of their behaviour;

- involve the victim in proceedings, but only with their active consent; and

- focus on preventing offending.

9.23   Detailed proposals are set out below. The new procedures would apply to young offenders aged 10 - 17 being sentenced by the youth court for the first time. They would not apply for serious offences, as set out in section 53 of the Children and Young Persons Act 1933, which should properly be dealt with at the Crown Court.

9.24   Implementation of this scheme would require primary legislation. The new approach would be piloted before full implementation, to ensure that the practical implications of the measures are fully tested, and the benefits of the new approach are maximised.

How would the new system work?

Not guilty pleas

9.25   If the young person pleaded not guilty, a trial would take place and the youth court would sentence the young person as now, making use of the full range of disposals available under the Crime and Disorder Bill. Conditional discharge would not be available - other than in exceptional circumstances - if the young person had received a Final Warning and re-offended within two years.

Guilty pleas: first time prosecutions

9.26   If the young person pleaded guilty, and it was their *first* court appearance, the youth court would convict the young person and, by way of disposal, refer him or her to a **youth panel**. In exceptional circumstances, where it was clear that although technically an offence had been committed no blame could be attached to the defendant, the court could instead issue an absolute discharge.

9.27   The youth panel would not be able to specify that the young person be held in custody. Magistrates would therefore be entitled, in exceptional cases, to retain a case in the youth court in order for the option of custody to be considered.

9.28   The youth panel members and the young person would have to draw up a 'contract', setting out clear requirements on the offender and on others, such as his or her parents. These requirements would ensure the young person made amends to the victim or the community at large and would tackle the causes of the offending behaviour.

9.29   The contract would always include an obligation to make **reparation**. This might be achieved through a letter of apology or a direct meeting with the victim; by putting right the damage caused by the offence; or through financial compensation. No reparation would be made to an individual victim without that victim's consent - in cases where a victim did not want direct reparation, offenders might instead be required to make amends to the community as a whole. In addition, the contract might include requirements to:

- participate in particular activities, such as family counselling sessions or drug rehabilitation courses;

- undertake unpaid work in the community;

- comply with educational arrangements, such as attending school or a training scheme; or

- refrain from doing certain things or going to particular places.

9.30   The youth court, when making the referral, would be able to specify how long it should last - which could be up to twelve months, depending on the seriousness of the offending. The youth panel would oversee the contract by way of reviews, conducted at least every three months.

9.31   Although the formal referral would be for a fixed period of time, the youth panel would be encouraged to identify ways of supporting the young person at the end of the referral through community based schemes such as mentoring, to help prevent further offending.

Enforcement

9.32   The contract would be enforced by the youth court. If the young person did not comply with the contract, he or she would be returned to the youth court to be sentenced for the original offence. The court would be able to impose any sentence which it could have imposed when the young person first appeared before it, but in doing so would have to take account of the extent to which the young offender had complied with the contract.

9.33   The young person would also be returned to the youth court for sentencing where the youth panel was unable to agree a contract with him or her.

9.34   If the young person kept to the agreed contract then when it was completed the youth court would be informed by way of a report and the justices' clerk would 'sign off' the contract. A young person's conviction would be regarded as being 'spent' for the purposes of the Rehabilitation of Offenders Act once the contract was signed off.

Attending a youth panel meeting

9.35   The youth panel would contain a mix of youth justice practitioners - a magistrate (if possible one of the magistrates responsible for the referral), a Youth Offending Team member, and perhaps a police officer. Appropriate training would be provided for members of the youth panel. It would be set up and serviced by the local Youth Offending Team, who would provide a clear summary of the original evidence and background information about the offender including, where appropriate, an account of any previous participation in a Final Warning intervention programme. The Youth Offending Team would also be responsible for bringing the case back to court if the young person failed to comply with the contract.

9.36   **Parents** of young offenders aged under 16 would be required to attend the panel session with the young person – unreasonable failure to do so would be a criminal offence. Parents of young offenders aged 16 and 17 would be encouraged to attend, where appropriate. Others, such as the young person's **teacher** and his or her **victim** (see paragraph 9.38), would also be able to attend the panel hearing. Arrangements might be made to hold panels in evenings, or weekends, to facilitate attendance.

9.37   There would be no legal representation at the youth panel stage. Guilt would already have been determined by the youth court, as would the length of the referral. The defendant would not be at risk of losing his or her liberty. Legal representation would put an obstacle in the way of the panel dealing directly with the defendant. If the young person were returned to the youth court for sentencing (because no contract could be agreed or because the contract was not completed), legal representation would be available.

Involving victims

9.38   Current sentencing arrangements often take little account of the views of victims or the wider community. Under the Government's new proposals, victims would be given every opportunity to participate in the discussions of the youth panels, though they would never be required against their will to meet an offender at a youth panel, or to have any other contact with the offender.

Conclusion

9.39   The Government's reforms of the youth court in England and Wales will help to shape a more effective youth justice system for the next century. The approach combines the principles of restorative justice with more traditional punitive measures, which must be available to the courts in order to protect the public. The overall result should be a more streamlined and effective system, with a clearer focus on preventing offending.

The proposals set out in this chapter represent major reform of the youth court. The Government would welcome views on the overall approach, and on the more detailed proposals for reform.